TRANSCENDENTAL
WILD OATS

TRANSCENDENTAL WILD OATS

AND EXCERPTS FROM THE FRUITLANDS DIARY

LOUISA MAY ALCOTT

WITH AN INTRODUCTION BY
WILLIAM HENRY HARRISON

AND ILLUSTRATIONS BY
J. STREETER FOWKE

THE HARVARD COMMON PRESS
BOSTON, MASSACHUSETTS

The Harvard Common Press
Boston, Massachusetts 02118

"Transcendental Wild Oats" was originally published in the
Independent, Vol. XXV, No. 1307 (December 18, 1873).
It was subsequently reprinted in the *Women's Journal*,
Vol. V, No. 8 (February 21, 1874); in *Silver Pitchers*;
Laurel Leaves. Original Poems, Stories, and Essays (Boston,
William Gill, 1876); and in *Golden Book Magazine*, Vol.
XIX, No. 112 (April, 1934).

Printed in the United States of America.

Library of Congress Cataloging in Publication data:

Alcott, Louisa May, 1832–1888.
   Transcendental wild oats and Excerpts from the
Fruitlands diary / by Louisa May Alcott; with an intro. by
William Henry Harrison; and ill. by J. Streeter Fowke.

I. Title: Transcendental wild oats. II. Title: Fruitlands diary.
PZ3.A355 Tr 5   813'.4   76-355426
[PS1017]   MARC

5 4 3

INTRODUCTION

FRUITLANDS AND
NEW ENGLAND TRANSCENDENTALISM

THE YEAR WAS 1843. SURELY THE MUSE OF Comedy presided over an old red farmhouse serenely situated at the foot of Prospect Hill in the remote and rural town of Harvard, Massachusetts, some dozen miles northwest of Concord.

This was to be a fateful year; corrupt sinful Earth was to be destroyed, according to the prophecies of Father William Miller. Only the good (i.e., the followers of Miller) were to be saved from the holocaust. This did not daunt a very small band of reformers led by Bronson Alcott and Charles Lane, eager for social and spiritual regeneration, from attempting the establishment of a utopia they called the Consociate Family in the red farmhouse which they named Fruitlands.

Louisa May Alcott's "Transcendental Wild Oats" is a fictionalized account of her father Bronson Alcott's utopian venture, the Fruitlands community. Louisa was only a child of ten when she came to Fruitlands; she became eleven on November 29, 1843. Thirty years after the abandonment of the idealistic venture, her story of the experiment was published.

Considering it a wild, harebrained scheme, Louisa pokes mild fun at Fruitlands' slightly madcap follies. She never grasped her father's ideology, a mystic and speculative philosophy; she made that clear when asked by Professor William Torrey Harris to write a biography of her father. "His philosophy I have never understood," she replied, "and biography is not in my line . . . . He has seen several of his ideals become facts and that is more than most of us ever do . . . ." [from a letter in the Fruitlands Museums Library]

Can "Transcendental Wild Oats" be taken as a reliable history of the Fruitlands community? Only in part. There is no question that absurdities such as Louisa recounts took place. This community (or "commune," as it would be known today) had its zany side; it attracted some freaks, cranks, and near lunatics. But there were also those who could be taken very seriously. In this story, the ludicrous obscures the serious intentions of the founders, Bronson Alcott and Charles Lane. One is reminded of Emerson's remark concerning some dubious, radical reform literature Alcott had sent him from England in 1842, the year before Fruitlands was established. "They speak to the conscience," Emerson commented, "and have that superiority over the crowd of their contemporaries, which belongs to men who entertain a good hope."

The final episode in Louisa's story, where Alcott takes to his bed in despair, was probably fabricated for a reading public with an insatiable appetite for the sentimental and melodramatic. The Victorian deathbed scene was popular, and Louisa presents it in full and mournful measure; but the present-day reader is tempted to smile instead of cry. That Bronson Alcott was depressed by the turn of events at Fruitlands is only natural. But we find no mention of this incident elsewhere, and the conduct described in this story does seem uncharacteristic of the ever-hopeful Alcott.

Despite her youth, Louisa was an astute

observer of life at Fruitlands, as is made very clear by the fragments that remain of the diary she kept when she was ten and eleven. (See pages 67 to 82 of this book.) Parts of this diary were published in Ednah D. Cheney's *Louisa May Alcott: Her Life, Letters, and Journals* (Boston: Roberts Brothers, 1889), but the diary itself, which Louisa allowed Mrs. Cheney to copy in part, was lost. Eight pages of the missing journal, however, were rediscovered in a house in Walpole, New Hampshire (where the Alcotts lived from 1855 to 1857), and were acquired by the Fruitlands Museums in 1973. These pages, never before published, appear herein and shed some new light on the history of Fruitlands.

New England Transcendentalism flourished from 1830 to 1880. A satisfactory definition of transcendentalism has long been the despair of historians and writers; one is tempted to use the definition of a Boston lady who remarked with a wave of the hand that transcendentalism meant "a little beyond." The more articulate Nathaniel Hawthorne thought a definition impossible—in "The Celestial Railroad" he satirizes transcendentalism as a terrible giant who "makes it his business to seize upon honest travellers and fatten them for his table with plentiful meals of smoke, mist, moonshine, raw potatoes, and sawdust. He is German by birth . . . but as to form, his features, his substance, and his nature generally, it is the chief peculiarity of this huge miscreant that neither he for himself, nor anybody for him, has ever been able to describe them."

The transcendental movement takes its name from a term used by Immanuel Kant in his *Critique of Pure Reason* (1781). Kant used "transcendental" to refer to ideas received by intuition instead of through the experience of the senses. This view was in opposition to the philosophy of Locke, who maintained that knowledge came via the senses. The "German philosophy," as it was called, was popularized in England by Coleridge, Wordsworth, and Carlyle, and was a part of the Romantic movement begun in the late eighteenth century, which spread very slowly to England and America. But as well as the idealistic German schools of thought, other philosophies, notably the neo-Platonian and the Oriental, flowed into transcendentalism.

The transcendentalist view of things, never a systematized doctrine or credo, was promulgated by adherents who made their views public through writings, lectures, and from the pulpit.

Theodore Parker (1810–1860), in his lecture *The Transcendentalist*, puts it simply. The transcendentalist, he says, believes "that man has faculties which transcend the senses; faculties which give him ideas and intuitions that transcend sensation experience; ideas whose origin is not from sensation, nor their proof from sensation." Old dogmas were cast off as shackles on mind and spirit. There was an exhilarating sense of freedom and new hope: the spirit could expand and soar into brighter realms. The thought of many of the transcendentalists was tinged with mysticism; Alcott himself was described as "the chief mystic of the transcendental band."

This movement had immense influence on American literature, criticism, thought, and art—freeing them from European conventions and direction. As Thomas Wentworth Higginson (1823–1911) remarks in his *Margaret Fuller Ossoli*:

> Behind all the catchwords, and even cant, if you please, of the Transcendentalists, lay the fact that they looked immediately around them for their stimulus, their scenery, their illustrations, and their properties. After fifty years of national life, the skylark and the nightingale were dethroned from our literature, and in the very first volume of the "Dial" the blue-bird and the woodthrush took their place. (p. 137)

The transcendentalists produced a voluminous literature: books, articles, translations, and several periodicals, chief of which was *The Dial*, published by Elizabeth P. Peabody.

A full understanding of New England transcendentalism calls for thoughtful reading of the writings of Ralph Waldo Emerson, Henry

David Thoreau, Bronson Alcott, Theodore Parker, Margaret Fuller, George Ripley, and Orestes Brownson, to mention only a few. It is interesting to note that in this movement women for the first time played an honored part in an American intellectual and spiritual movement.

Clearly transcendentalism had its full share of worthy persons taking active parts as rank-and-file supporters and as propagandists. But reform movements often suffer from a lunatic fringe, and the "newness" (a popular name for transcendentalism) was no exception. Those who were persuaded that the spirit was the sole guide to correct conduct gave their spirits free rein, giving rise to numberless gossipy stories. The very word "transcendentalism" became synonymous with flighty, ethereal vacuities and comic antics. High purpose and thoughtful action were beclouded by a reputation for vagary and absurdity.

The characters presented to us in "Transcendental Wild Oats" are caricatures of such transcendentalists, rendered broadly as Louisa spoofs their impractical utopian ideals. Short sketches follow of three major historical figures she satirizes:

Amos Bronson Alcott (Abel Lamb of "Transcendental Wild Oats") was 43 when he founded the Consociate Family at Fruitlands in Harvard, Massachusetts. Born and brought up on a Connecticut farm, he was attracted to schoolteaching and developed a sincere interest in improving schools for young children—"infant education," as he called it. He early established a reputation in this field, and became known by the soubriquet "the American Pestalozzi." Alcott's aim was to interest children, furnish attractive schoolrooms, and make education more inviting than formidable; his best-known school was located in rooms in the Masonic Temple in Boston.

On his move to Concord, Alcott found in Ralph Waldo Emerson a warm neighbor, very responsive to his ideas. Emerson often came to the aid of his impecunious friend, and gave him much moral support as well; but he was not keen about the Fruitlands venture, thinking it could only end in failure. On July 4, 1843, Emerson visited Fruitlands and entered the cautious remark in his journal: "I will not prejudge them successful. They look well in July. We shall see them in December."

Though Emerson was fascinated by Alcott's talk, he was well aware of his friend's deficiencies. Alcott was never a good writer; the glow went out of his words when committed to cold white paper. Too often, Alcott's ideas took shape in the dark terms of the philosophy of mysticism.

Alcott's "image" takes on protean shapes. To some he is a great man, a seer, and a sage. Others think him hopelessly impractical and dreamy, if not a charlatan. Present-day scholars judge Alcott more favorably. Professor Austin Warren, for example, writes in his *New England Saints* (1956), "Bronson Alcott—probably the most representative, certainly the most picturesque among the New England Transcendentalists—does not deserve to reach posterity as the impractical parent of a story-teller for girls.

Bronson Alcott
(Courtesy Orchard House, Concord, Massachusetts)

Though a butt for the satire of the Philistine among his contemporaries, he won and held the respect of the intellectuals of his day both as man and as thinker."

Typical of critics priding themselves on a no-nonsense attitude toward Alcott was E. W. Howe, the country editor who achieved a national reputation for his biting *Monthly*. Devoting an entire chapter of his *Ventures in Common Sense* (1919) to cutting Bronson Alcott down to size, he sadly concludes: "The world is full of Bronson Alcotts to-day. You may find a Bronson Alcott in every community; a nuisance, yet loudly announcing that he is superior to useful, sensible and worthy people. Why should we make heroes of these foolish men? Why not declare the truth about them now, instead of hereafter? Why submit to their untruthful and foolish abuse? Why submit to the unnecessary trouble they cause?"*

---

* It remained for an Englishman, a brilliant young scholar now at Manchester University, to produce the first serious study of the philosophical and social ideas that underlay the views of the founders of Fruitlands,

Charles Lane (Timon Lion of "Transcendental Wild Oats") was an English businessman and a reformer, a mystic and a transcendentalist. Alcott had met him when he visited Alcott House, Ham Common, England, a school based on his own educational principles and associated with the communal venture known as the Concordium. With his son William, aged 10, and H. G. Wright, a teacher at Alcott House, Lane joined Alcott on his return to America in the autumn of 1842—their avowed intention to establish a community. They were bent, as Thomas Carlyle put it in a letter to Emerson, "on saving the world by a return to acorns and the golden age."

Lane was no blithe spirit, not the man for a light moment. A daguerreotype portrait reveals a grim, tightlipped, lean-faced man. It is the face of a disciplinarian; and Lane's writings,

---

Bronson Alcott and Charles Lane (Richard Francis: "Circumstances and Salvation: The Ideology of the Fruitlands Utopia." *American Quarterly* 25:202–234, May 1973).

Charles Lane
(Courtesy of the Fruitlands Museums, Harvard, Massachusetts)

mostly on reform topics, are as stiff and angular as his visage.

On arrival in Concord, Lane threw the Alcott household into turmoil, for gradually, to the dismay of Mrs. Alcott and the girls, he placed them under a strict daily regimen that continued until the abandonment of the Fruitlands experiment. Mrs. Alcott laconically reports his departure from Fruitlands in her diary on January 6, 1844: "Mr. Lane leaves with William for the Shakers at Harvard."

Lane was to find life with the celibate Shakers uncongenial. For a short time he tried another communal venture at Red Bank, New Jersey, but returned to England in 1846 and remarried, fathering five children despite his former view that marriage was a stumbling block to the True Life.

Wistfully Lane looked back on Fruitlands and considered writing a history of the experiment; but like the other participants, he never got around to it. That task remained for the irrepressible Louisa, the only participant of Fruitlands ever to present a first-hand view of the community.

Joseph Palmer (Moses White of "Transcendental Wild Oats") of Fitchburg and No Town, flaunted the most celebrated beard in America. Palmer stoutly defended his right to wear the beard—an adornment low in public esteem in the 1830s—and rather than pay a small fine he spent a year in the Worcester jail. This difficult period is carefully recorded in his diary, now in the Fruitlands Museums Library. God in His wisdom had given him the beard, Palmer said, and who was mortal man to undo the work of the Almighty?

He brought to Fruitlands its only element of the practical, taking charge of the farm and supplying the necessary gear. "Spade culture" had proved hard on philosophers' hands and untried muscles, so Palmer took over the work with a plow drawn by an ox and a cow. To supplement the spare Fruitlands diet, he secretly milked that cow—depriving it, his fellows charged, of its natural right to its milk!

After Fruitlands was abandoned, Palmer bought the property from Emerson, who had held it as trustee and who later acted in its

The grave of Joseph Palmer, "*persecuted for
wearing the beard.*"
(Courtesy of the Fruitlands Museums, Harvard, Massachusetts)

disposal as agent for Charles Lane, cofounder of the Consociate Family. Renamed "Freelands" by its new owner, the house became a kind of hostel for waifs, tramps, and stray characters of all descriptions.

The transition from "Fruitlands" to "Apple Slump" was not as dramatic an event as Louisa describes it. To all appearances the community was prospering in midsummer; but gradually rifts occurred. One by one, all the persons who had joined the community left for one reason or another—chiefly, wrote Lane, because of Alcott's "despotic manner." To Alcott, it seemed that the others were unable to meet "the Spirit's demands." In addition Alcott and Lane had sauntered off on a number of proselytizing excursions when their attention should have been directed to the crops. And finally, increasingly antagonistic views developed between the two founders. Lane came to regard marriage as an impediment to the nobler life and urged on Alcott the adoption of celibacy and the dissolution of the family. These opinions were contradicted by those of his wife; Alcott stood in a crisis of indecision. At last, Lane went to the Shakers, with whose view of the sexes he sympathized; and Alcott, firmly united with his family, removed to a nearby farmhouse and a little later to the village of Still River.

Though an economic failure, Fruitlands was not necessarily a spiritual one. The experiment marked a departure from all other schemes of communal living, for it embodied Alcott's central conviction that all effective and enduring changes in society must originate "within the individual and work outwards." It was with Fruitlands as it has been with many another ambitious radical scheme for the reorganization of society, a constant see-saw of the ridiculous and the sublime.

William Henry Harrison
Director, Fruitlands Museums
November 1, 1975

Transcendental Wild Oats

A Chapter from an Unwritten Romance

The characters in *Transcendental Wild Oats* and
their counterparts in the Fruitlands Community:

Abel Lamb . . . . Bronson Alcott

Timon Lion . . . . Charles Lane

Hope Lamb . . . . Mrs. Alcott

Her Daughters . . . . . . Anna, Louisa, Elizabeth, and May

Son of Timon Lion . . . . William Lane

Moses White . . . . Joseph Palmer

John Pease . . . . Samuel Bower

Wood Abram . . . . Abram Wood

Forest Absalom . . . . Abraham Everett

Jane Gage . . . . Anne Page

ON THE FIRST DAY OF JUNE, 184–, A LARGE wagon, drawn by a small horse and containing a motley load, went lumbering over certain New England hills, with the pleasing accompaniments of wind, rain, and hail. A serene man with a serene child upon his knee was driving, or rather being driven, for the small horse had it all his own way. A brown boy with a William Penn style of countenance sat beside him, firmly embracing a bust of Socrates. Behind them was an energetic-looking woman, with a benevolent brow, satirical mouth, and eyes brimful of hope and courage. A baby reposed upon her lap, a mirror leaned against her knee, and a basket of provisions danced about at her feet, as she struggled with a large, unruly umbrella. Two blue-eyed little girls, with hands full of childish treasures, sat under one old shawl, chatting happily together.

In front of this lively party stalked a tall, sharp-featured man, in a long blue cloak; and a fourth small girl trudged along beside him through the mud as if she rather enjoyed it.

The wind whistled over the bleak hills; the rain fell in a despondent drizzle, and twilight began to fall. But the calm man gazed as tranquilly into the fog as if he beheld a radiant bow of promise spanning the gray sky. The cheery woman tried to cover every one but herself with the big umbrella. The brown boy pillowed his head on the bald pate of Socrates and slumbered peacefully. The little girls sang lullabies to their dolls in soft, maternal murmurs. The sharp-nosed pedestrian marched steadily on, with the blue cloak streaming out behind him like a banner; and the lively infant splashed through the puddles with a duck-like satisfaction pleasant to behold.

Thus these modern pilgrims journeyed hopefully out of the old world, to found a new one in the wilderness.

The editors of *The Transcendental Tripod* had received from Messrs. Lion & Lamb (two of the aforesaid pilgrims) a communication from which the following statement is an extract:

"We have made arrangements with the proprietor of an estate of about a hundred acres which liberates this tract from human ownership. Here we shall prosecute our effort to initiate a Family in harmony with the primitive instincts of man.

"Ordinary secular farming is not our object. Fruit, grain, pulse, herbs, flax, and other vegetable products, receiving assiduous attention, will afford ample manual occupation, and chaste supplies for the bodily needs. It is intended to adorn the pastures with orchards, and to supersede the labor of cattle by the spade and the pruning-knife.

"Consecrated to human freedom, the land awaits the sober culture of devoted men. Beginning with small pecuniary means, this enterprise must be rooted in a reliance on the succors of an ever-bounteous Providence, whose vital affinities being secured by this union with uncorrupted field and unworldly persons, the cares and injuries of a life of gain are avoided.

"The inner nature of each member of the Family is at no time neglected. Our plan contemplates all such disciplines, cultures, and habits as evidently conduce to the purifying of the inmates.

"Pledged to the spirit alone, the founders anticipate no hasty or numerous addition to their numbers. The kingdom of peace is entered only through the gates of self-denial; and felicity is the test and the reward of loyalty to the unswerving law of Love."

This prospective Eden at present consisted of an old red farm-house, a dilapidated barn, many acres of meadow-land, and a grove. Ten ancient apple trees were all the "chaste supply" which the place offered as yet; but, in the firm belief that plenteous orchards were soon to be evoked from their inner consciousness, these sanguine founders had christened their domain Fruitlands.

Here Timon Lion intended to found a colony of Latter Day Saints, who, under his patriarchal sway, should regenerate the world and glorify his name for ever. Here Abel Lamb, with the devoutest faith in the high ideal which was to him a living truth, desired to plant a

Fruitlands

Paradise, where Beauty, Virtue, Justice, and Love might live happily together, without the possibility of a serpent entering in. And here his wife, unconverted but faithful to the end, hoped, after many wanderings over the face of the earth, to find rest for herself and a home for her children.

"There is our new abode," announced the enthusiast, smiling with a satisfaction quite un-damped by the drops dripping from his hat-brim, as they turned at length into a cart-path that wound along a steep hillside into a barren-looking valley.

"A little difficult of access," observed his practical wife, as she endeavored to keep her various household gods from going overboard with every lurch of the laden ark.

"Like all good things. But those who earnestly desire and patiently seek will soon find us," placidly responded the philosopher from the mud, through which he was now endeavoring to pilot the much-enduring horse.

"Truth lies at the bottom of a well, Sister Hope," said Brother Timon, pausing to detach his small comrade from a gate, whereon she was perched for a clearer gaze into futurity.

"That's the reason we so seldom get at it, I suppose," replied Mrs. Hope, making a vain clutch at the mirror, which a sudden jolt sent flying out of her hands.

"We want no false reflections here," said Timon, with a grim smile, as he crunched the fragments under foot in his onward march.

Sister Hope held her peace, and looked wistfully through the mist at her promised home. The old red house with a hospitable glimmer at its windows cheered her eyes; and, considering the weather, was a fitter refuge than the sylvan bowers some of the more ardent souls might have preferred.

The newcomers were welcomed by one of the elect precious—a regenerate farmer, whose idea of reform consisted chiefly in wearing white cotten raiment and shoes of untanned leather. This costume, with a snowy beard, gave him a venerable, and at the same time a somewhat bridal appearance.

The goods and chattels of the Society not having arrived, the weary family reposed before the fire on blocks of wood, while Brother Moses White regaled them with roasted potatoes, brown bread and water, in two plates, a tin pan, and one mug—his table service being limited. But, having cast the forms and vanities of a depraved world behind them, the elders welcomed hardship with the enthusiasm of new pioneers, and the children heartily enjoyed this foretaste of what they believed was to be a sort of perpetual picnic.

During the progress of this frugal meal, two

more brothers appeared. One a dark, melancholy man, clad in homespun, whose particular mission was to turn his name hind part before and use as few words as possible. The other was a bland, bearded Englishman, who expected to be saved by eating uncooked food and going without clothes. He had not yet adopted the primitive costume, however; but contented himself with meditatively chewing dry beans out of a basket.

"Every meal should be a sacrament, and the vessels used beautiful and symbolical," observed Brother Lamb, mildly, righting the tin pan slipping about on his knees. "I priced a silver service when in town, but it was too costly; so I got some graceful cups and vases of Britannia ware."

"Hardest things in the world to keep bright. Will whiting be allowed in the community?" inquired Sister Hope, with a housewife's interest in labor-saving institutions.

"Such trivial questions will be discussed at a more fitting time," answered Brother Timon, sharply, as he burnt his fingers with a very hot potato. "Neither sugar, molasses, milk, butter, cheese, nor flesh are to be used among us, for nothing is to be admitted which has caused wrong or death to man or beast."

"Our garments are to be linen till we learn to raise our own cotton or some substitute for woollen fabrics," added Brother Abel, blissfully basking in an imaginary future as warm and brilliant as the generous fire before him.

"Haou abaout shoes?" asked Brother Moses, surveying his own with interest.

"We must yield that point till we can manufacture an innocent substitute for leather. Bark, wood, or some durable fabric will be invented in time. Meanwhile, those who desire to carry out our idea to the fullest extent can go barefooted," said Lion, who liked extreme measures.

"I never will, nor let my girls," murmured rebellious Sister Hope, under her breath.

"Haou do you cattle'ate to treat the ten-acre lot? Ef things ain't 'tended to right smart, we shan't hev no crops," observed the practical patriarch in cotton.

"We shall spade it," replied Abel, in such perfect good faith that Moses said no more, though he indulged in a shake of the head as he glanced at hands that had held nothing heavier than a pen for years. He was a paternal old soul and regarded the younger men as promising boys on a new sort of lark.

"What shall we do for lamps, if we cannot use any animal substance? I do hope light of some sort is to be thrown upon the enterprise," said Mrs. Lamb, with anxiety, for in those days kerosene and camphene were not, and gas unknown in the wilderness.

"We shall go without till we have discovered some vegetable oil or wax to serve us," replied Brother Timon, in a decided tone, which caused Sister Hope to resolve that her private lamp should always be trimmed, if not burning.

"Each member is to perform the work for which experience, strength, and taste best fit him," continued Dictator Lion. "Thus drudgery and disorder will be avoided and harmony prevail. We shall arise at dawn, begin the day by bathing, followed by music, and then a chaste repast of fruit and bread. Each one finds congenial occupation till the meridian meal; when some deep-searching conversation gives rest to the body and development to the mind. Healthful labor again engages us till the last meal, when we assemble in social communion, prolonged till sunset, when we retire to sweet repose, ready for the next day's activity."

"What part of the work do you incline to yourself?" asked Sister Hope, with a humorous glimmer in her keen eyes.

"I shall wait till it is made clear to me. Being in preference to doing is the great aim, and this comes to us rather by a resigned willingness than a willful activity, which is a check to all divine growth," responded Brother Timon.

"I thought so." And Mrs. Lamb sighed audibly, for during the year he had spent in her family Brother Timon had so faithfully carried out his idea of "being, not doing," that she had found his "divine growth" both an expensive and unsatisfactory process.

Here her husband struck into the conversation, his face shining with the light and joy of the splendid dreams and high ideals hovering before him.

"In these steps of reform, we do not rely so much on scientific reasoning or physiological skill as on the spirit's dictates. The greater part of man's duty consists in leaving alone much that he now does. Shall I stimulate with tea, coffee, or wine? No. Shall I consume flesh? Not if I value health. Shall I subjugate cattle? Shall I claim property in any created thing? Shall I trade? Shall I adopt a form of religion? Shall I interest myself in politics? To how many of these questions—could we ask them deeply enough and could they be heard as having relation to our eternal welfare—would the response be 'Abstain'?"

A mild snore seemed to echo the last word of Abel's rhapsody, for brother Moses had succumbed to mundane slumber and sat nodding like a massive ghost. Forest Absalom, the silent man, and John Pease, the English member, now departed to the barn; and Mrs. Lamb led her flock to a temporary fold, leaving the founders of the "Consociate Family" to build castles in the air till the fire went out and the symposium ended in smoke.

The furniture arrived next day, and was soon bestowed; for the principal property of the community consisted in books. To this rare library was devoted the best room in the house, and the few busts and pictures that still survived many flittings were added to beautify the sanctuary, for here the family was to meet for amusement, instruction, and worship.

Any housewife can imagine the emotions of Sister Hope, when she took possession of a large, dilapidated kitchen, containing an old stove and the peculiar stores out of which food was to be evolved for her little family of eleven. Cakes of maple sugar, dried peas and beans, barley and hominy, meal of all sorts, potatoes, and dried fruit. No milk, butter, cheese, tea, or meat, appeared. Even salt was considered a useless luxury and spice entirely forbidden by these lovers of Spartan simplicity. A ten years' experience of vegetarian vagaries had been

The long kitchen

good training for this new freak, and her sense of the ludicrous supported her through many trying scenes.

Unleavened bread, porridge, and water for breakfast; bread, vegetables, and water for dinner; bread, fruit, and water for supper was the bill of fare ordained by the elders. No teapot profaned that sacred stove, no gory steak cried aloud for vengeance from her chaste gridiron;

and only a brave woman's taste, time, and temper were sacrificed on that domestic altar.

The vexed question of light was settled by buying a quantity of bayberry wax for candles; and, on discovering that no one knew how to make them, pine knots were introduced, to be used when absolutely necessary. Being summer, the evenings were not long, and the weary fraternity found it no great hardship to retire with the birds. The inner light was sufficient for most of them. But Mrs. Lamb rebelled. Evening was the only time she had to herself, and while the tired feet rested the skilful hands mended torn frocks and little stockings, or anxious heart forgot its burden in a book.

So "mother's lamp" burned steadily, while the philosophers built a new heaven and earth by moonlight; and through all the metaphysical mists and philanthropic pyrotechnics of that period Sister Hope played her own little game of "throwing light," and none but the moths were the worse for it.

Such farming probably was never seen before since Adam delved. The band of brothers began by spading garden and field; but a few days of it lessened their ardor amazingly. Blistered hands and aching backs suggested the expediency of permitting the use of cattle till the workers were better fitted for noble toil by a summer of the new life.

Brother Moses brought a yoke of oxen from his farm—at least, the philosophers thought so till it was discovered that one of the animals was a cow; and Moses confessed that he "must be let down easy, for he couldn't live on garden sarse entirely."

Great was Dictator Lion's indignation at this lapse from virtue. But time pressed, the work must be done; so the meek cow was permitted to wear the yoke and the recreant brother continued to enjoy forbidden draughts in the barn, which dark proceeding caused the children to regard him as one set apart for destruction.

The sowing was equally peculiar, for, owing to some mistake, the three brethren, who devoted themselves to this graceful task, found when about half through the job that each had been sowing a different sort of grain in the same field; a mistake which caused much perplexity, as it could not be remedied; but, after a long consultation and a good deal of laughter, it was decided to say nothing and see what would come of it.

The garden was planted with a generous supply of useful roots and herbs; but, as manure was not allowed to profane the virgin soil, few of these vegetable treasures ever came up. Purslane reigned supreme, and the disappointed planters ate it philosophically, deciding that Nature knew what was best for them, and would generously supply their needs, if they could only learn to digest her "sallets" and wild roots.

The orchard was laid out, a little grafting done, new trees and vines set, regardless of the unfit season and entire ignorance of the husbandmen, who honestly believed that in the autumn they would reap a bounteous harvest.

Slowly things got into order, and rapidly rumors of the new experiment went abroad, causing many strange spirts to flock thither, for in those days communities were the fashion and transcendentalism raged wildly. Some came to look on and laugh, some to be supported in poetic idleness, a few to believe sincerely and work heartily. Each member was allowed to mount his favorite hobby and ride it to his heart's content. Very queer were some of the riders, and very rampant some of the hobbies.

One youth, believing that language was of little consequence if the spirit was only right, startled newcomers by blandly greeting them with "good morning, damn you,"* and other remarks of an equally mixed order. A second irrepressible being held that all the emotions of the soul should be freely expressed, and illustrated his theory by antics that would have

---

* In the earliest published version of "Transcendental Wild Oats," in the *Independent* on December 18, 1873, this sentence reads: ". . . by blandly greetng them with 'Good-morning,' appending an anathema." The *Independent*'s editors apparently edited the phrase to protect their readers' sensibilities.

sent him to a lunatic asylum, if, as an unregen-
erate wag said, he had not already been in one.
When his spirit soared, he climbed trees and
shouted; when doubt assailed him, he lay upon
the floor and groaned lamentably. At joyful
periods, he raced, leaped, and sang; when sad,
he wept aloud; and when a great thought burst
upon him in the watches of the night, he
crowed like a jocund cockerel, to the great
delight of the children and the great an-
noyance of the elders. One musical brother fid-
dled whenever so moved, sang sentimentally to
the four little girls, and put a music-box on the
wall when he hoed corn.

Brother Pease ground away at his uncooked food, or browsed over the farm on sor-
rel, mint, green fruit, and new vegetables.
Occasionally he took his walks abroad, airily
attired in an unbleached cotton *poncho*, which
was the nearest approach to the primeval costume he was allowed to indulge in. At midsummer he retired to the wilderness, to try his plan
where the woodchucks were without prejudices
and huckleberry bushes were hospitably full. A

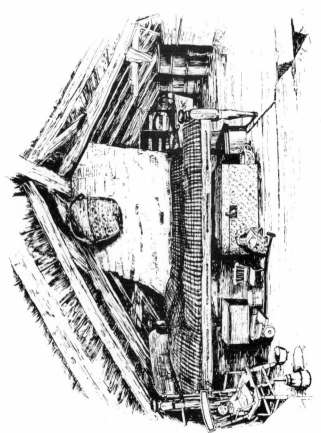

The girls' attic bedroom

sunstroke unfortunately spoilt his plan, and he returned to semi-civilization a sadder and wiser man.

Forest Absalom preserved his Pythagorean silence, cultivated his fine dark locks, and worked like a beaver, setting an excellent example of brotherly love, justice, and fidelity by his upright life. He it was who helped overworked Sister Hope with her heavy washes, kneaded the endless succession of batches of bread, watched over the children, and did the many tasks left undone by the brethren, who were so busy discussing and defining great duties that they forgot to perform the small ones.

Moses White placidly plodded about, "chorin' raound," as he called it, looking like an old-time patriarch, with his silver hair and flowing beard, and saving the community from many a mishap by his thrift and Yankee shrewdness.

Brother Lion domineered over the whole concern; for, having put the most money into the speculation, he was resolved to make it pay—as if anything founded on an ideal basis could be expected to do so by any but enthusiasts.

Abel Lamb simply revelled in the Newness, firmly believing that his dream was to be beautifully realized, and in time not only little Fruitlands, but the whole earth, be turned into a Happy Valley. He worked with every muscle of his body, for *he* was in deadly earnest. He taught with his whole head and heart; planned and sacrificed, preached and prophesied, with a soul full of the purest aspirations, most unselfish purposes, and desires for a life devoted to God and man, too high and tender to bear the rough usage of this world.

It was a little remarkable that only one woman ever joined this community. Mrs. Lamb merely followed wheresoever her husband led—"as ballast for his balloon," as she said, in her bright way.

Miss Jane Gage was a stout lady of mature years, sentimental, amiable, and lazy. She wrote verses copiously, and had vague yearnings and graspings after the unknown, which led her to believe herself fitted for a higher sphere than any she had yet adorned.

Having been a teacher, she was set to instructing the children in the common branches. Each adult member took a turn at the infants; and, as each taught in his own way, the result was a chronic state of chaos in the minds of these much-afflicted innocents.

Sleep, food, and poetic musings were the desires of dear Jane's life, and she shirked all duties as clogs upon her spirit's wings. Any thought of lending a hand with the domestic drudgery never occurred to her; and when to the question, "Are there any beasts of burden on the place?" Mrs. Lamb answered, with a face that told its own tale, "Only one woman!" the buxom Jane took no shame to herself, but laughed at the joke, and let the stout-hearted sister tug on alone.

Unfortunately, the poor lady hankered after the fleshpots, and endeavored to stay herself with private sips of milk, crackers, and cheese, and on one dire occasion she partook of fish at a neighbor's table.

One of the children reported this sad lapse from virtue, and poor Jane was publicly reprimanded by Timon.

"I only took a little bit of the tail," sobbed the penitent poetess.

"Yes, but the whole fish had to be tortured and slain that you might tempt your carnal appetite with that one taste of the tail. Know ye not, consumers of flesh meat, that ye are nourishing the wolf and tiger in your bosoms?"

At this awful question and the peal of laughter which arose from some of the younger brethren, tickled by the ludicrous contrast between the stout sinner, the stern judge, and the naughty satisfaction of the young detective, poor Jane fled from the room to pack her trunk, and return to a world where fishes' tails were not forbidden fruit.

Transcendental wild oats were sown broadcast that year, and the fame thereof has not yet ceased in the land; for, futile as this crop seemed to outsiders, it bore an invisible harvest, worth much to those who planted in earnest. As none of the members of this particular community have ever recounted their experiences before, a few of them may not be amiss, since the interest in these attempts has never died out and Fruitlands was the most ideal of all these castles in Spain.

A new dress was invented, since cotton, silk, and wool were forbidden as the product of slave-labor, worm-slaughter, and sheep-robbery. Tunics and trowsers of brown linen were the only wear. The women's skirts were longer, and their straw hat-brims wider than the men's, and this was the only difference. Some persecution lent a charm to the costume, and the long-haired, linen-clad reformers quite enjoyed the mild martyrdom they endured when they left home.

Money was abjured, as the root of all evil. The produce of the land was to supply most of their wants, or be exchanged for the few things they could not grow. This idea had its inconveniences; but self-denial was the fashion, and it was surprising how many things one can do without. When they desired to travel, they walked, if possible, begged the loan of a vehicle, or boldly entered car or coach, and, stating their principles to the officials, took the consequences. Usually their dress, their earnest frankness, and gentle resolution won them a passage; but now and then they met with hard usage, and had the satisfaction of suffering for their principles.

On one of these penniless pilgrimages they took passage on a boat, and, when fare was demanded, artlessly offered to talk, instead of pay. As the boat was well under way and they actually had not a cent, there was no help for it. So Brothers Lion and Lamb held forth to the assembled passengers in their most eloquent style. There must have been something effective in this conversation, for the listeners were moved to take up a contribution for these inspired lunatics, who preached peace on earth and goodwill to man so earnestly, with empty pockets. A goodly sum was collected; but when the captain presented it the reformers proved that they were consistent even in their madness, for not a penny would they accept, saying, with a look at the group about them,

The study

whose indifference or contempt had changed
to interest and respect, "You see how well we
get on without money;" and so went serenely
on their way, with their linen blouses flapping
airily in the cold October wind.

They preached vegetarianism everywhere
and resisted all temptations of the flesh, con-
tentedly eating apples and bread at well-spread

tables, and much afflicting hospitable hostesses by denouncing their food and taking away their appetites, discussing the "horrors of shambles," the "incorporation of the brute in man," and "on elegant abstinence the sign of a pure soul." But, when the perplexed or offended ladies asked what they should eat, they got in reply a bill of fare consisting of "bowls of sunrise for breakfast," "solar seeds of the sphere," "dishes from Plutarch's chaste table," and other viands equally hard to find in any modern market.

Reform conventions of all sorts were haunted by these brethren, who said many wise things and did many foolish ones. Unfortunately, these wanderings interfered with their harvest at home; but the rule was to do what the spirit moved, so they left their crops to Providence and went a-reaping in wider and, let us hope, more fruitful fields than their own.

Luckily, the earthly providence who watched over Abel Lamb was at hand to glean the scanty crop yielded by the "uncorrupted land," which, "consecrated to human freedom," had received "the sober culture of devout men."

About the time the grain was ready to house, some call of the Oversoul wafted all the men away. An easterly storm was coming up and the yellow stacks were sure to be ruined. Then Sister Hope gathered her forces. Three little girls, one boy (Timon's son), and herself, harnessed to clothes-baskets and Russia-linen sheets, were the only teams she could command; but with these poor appliances the indomitable woman got in the grain and saved food for her young, with the instinct and energy of a mother-bird with a brood of hungry nestlings to feed.

This attempt at regeneration had its tragic as well as comic side, though the world only saw the former.

With the first frosts, the butterflies, who had sunned themselves in the new light through the summer, took flight, leaving the few bees to see what honey they had stored for winter use. Precious little appeared beyond the satisfaction of a few months of holy living.

At first it seemed as if a chance to try holy dying was also to be offered them. Timon, much disgusted with the failure of the scheme, decided to retire to the Shakers, who seemed to be the only successful community going.

"What is to become of us?" asked Mrs. Hope, for Abel was heartbroken at the bursting of his lovely bubble.

"You can stay here, if you like, till a tenant is found. No more wood must be cut, however, and no more corn ground. All I have must be sold to pay the debts of the concern, as the responsibility is mine," was the cheering reply.

"Who is to pay us for what we have lost? I gave all I had—furniture, time, strength, six months of my children's lives—and all are wasted. Abel gave himself body and soul, and is almost wrecked by hard work and disappointment. Are we to have no return for this, but leave to starve and freeze in an old house, with winter at hand, no money, and hardly a friend left, for this wild scheme has alienated nearly all we had. You talk much about justice. Let us have a little, since there is nothing else left."

But the woman's appeal met with no reply but the old one: "It was an experiment. We all risked something, and must bear our losses as we can."

With this cold comfort, Timon departed with his son, and was absorbed into the Shaker brotherhood, where he soon found that the order of things was reversed, and it was all work and no play.

Then the tragedy began for the forsaken little family. Desolation and despair fell upon Abel. As his wife said, his new beliefs had alienated many friends. Some thought him mad, some unprincipled. Even the most kindly thought him a visionary, whom it was useless to help till he took more practical views of life. All stood aloof, saying: "Let him work out his own ideas, and see what they are worth."

He had tried, but it was a failure. The world was not ready for Utopia yet, and those who attempted to found it only got laughed at for their pains. In other days, men could sell all and give to the poor, lead lives devoted to holiness and high thought, and after the persecution was over, find themselves honored as saints or martyrs. But in modern times these things are out of fashion. To live for one's principles, at all costs, is a dangerous speculation; and the failure of an ideal, no matter how humane and noble, is harder for the world to forgive and forget than bank robbery or the grand swindles of corrupt politicians.

Deep waters now for Abel, and for a time there seemed no passage through. Strength and spirits were exhausted by hard work and too much thought. Courage failed when, looking about for help, he saw no sympathizing face, no hand outstretched to help him, no voice to say cheerily:

"We all make mistakes, and it takes many experiences to shape a life. Try again, and let us help you."

Every door was closed, every eye averted, every heart cold, and no way open whereby he might earn bread for his children. His principles would not permit him to do many things that others did; and in the few fields where conscience would allow him to work, who would employ a man who had flown in the face of society, as he had done?

Then this dreamer, whose dream was the life of his life, resolved to carry out his idea to the bitter end. There seemed no place for him here—no work, no friend. To go begging conditions was as ignoble as to go begging money. Better perish of want than sell one's soul for the sustenance of his body. Silently he lay down upon his bed, turned his face to the wall, and waited with pathetic patience for death to cut the knot which he could not untie. Days and nights went by, and neither food nor water passed his lips. Soul and body were dumbly struggling together, and no word of complaint betrayed what either suffered.

His wife, when tears and prayers were unavailing, sat down to wait the end with a mysterious awe and submission; for in this entire resignation of all things there was an eloquent significance to her who knew him as no other human being did.

"Leave all to God," was his belief; and in this crisis the loving soul clung to his faith, sure that the All-wise Father would not desert this child who tried to live so near to Him. Gathering her children about her, she waited the issue of the tragedy that was being enacted in that solitary room, while the first snow fell outside, untrodden by the footprints of a single friend.

But the strong angels who sustain and teach perplexed and troubled souls came and went, leaving no trace without, but working miracles within. For, when all other sentiments had faded into dimness, all other hopes died utterly; when the bitterness of death was nearly

The Alcott bedroom

over, when the body was past any pang of hunger or thirst, and soul stood ready to depart, the love that outlives all else refused to die. Head had bowed to defeat, hand had grown weary with too heavy tasks, but heart could not grow cold to those who live in its tender depths, even when death touched it.

"My faithful wife, my little girls—they have not forsaken me, they are mine by ties that none can break. What right have I to leave them alone? What right to escape from the burden and the sorrow I have helped to bring? This duty remains to me, and I must do it manfully. For their sakes, the world will forgive me in time; for their sakes, God will sustain me now."

Too feeble to rise, Abel groped for the food that always lay within his reach, and in the darkness and solitude of that memorable night ate and drank what was to him the bread and wine of a new communion, a new dedication of heart and life to the duties that were left him when the dreams fled.

In the early dawn, when that sad wife crept

fearfully to see what change had come to the patient face on the pillow, she found it smiling at her, saw a wasted hand outstretched to her, and heard a feeble voice cry bravely, "Hope!"

What passed in that little room is not to be recorded except in the hearts of those who suffered and endured much for love's sake. Enough for us to know that soon the wan shadow of a man came forth, leaning on the arm that never failed him, to be welcomed and cherished by the children, who never forgot the experiences of that time.

"Hope" was the watchword now; and, while the last logs blazed on the hearth, the last bread and apples covered the table, the new commander, with recovered courage, said to her husband:

"Leave all to God—and me. He has done his part; now I will do mine."

"But we have no money, dear."

"Yes, we have. I sold all we could spare, and have enough to take us away from this snowbank."

"Where can we go?"

"I have engaged four rooms at our good neighbor, Lovejoy's. There we can live cheaply till spring. Then for new plans and a home of our own, please God."

"But, Hope, your little store won't last long, and we have no friends."

"I can sew and you can chop wood. Lovejoy offers you the same pay as he gives his other men; my old friend, Mrs. Truman, will send me all the work I want; and my blessed brother stands by us to the end. Cheer up, dear heart, for while there is work and love in the world we shall not suffer."

"And while I have my good angel Hope, I shall not despair, even if I wait another thirty years before I step beyond the circle of the sacred little world in which I still have a place to fill."

So one bleak December day, with their few possessions piled on an ox-sled, the rosy children perched atop, and the parents trudging arm in arm behind, the exiles left their Eden and faced the world again.

"Ah, me! my happy dream. How much I

leave behind that never can be mine again," said Abel, looking back at the lost Paradise, lying white and chill in its shroud of snow.

"Yes, dear; but how much we bring away," answered brave-hearted Hope, glancing from husband to children.

"Poor Fruitlands! The name was as great a failure as the rest!" continued Abel, with a sigh, as a frost-bitten apple fell from a leafless bough at his feet.

But the sigh changed to a smile as his wife added, in a half-tender, half-satirical tone:

"Don't you think Apple Slump would be a better name for it, dear?"

The Fruitlands Diary

of Louisa May Alcott

Louisa May Alcott
(Courtesy Orchard House, Concord, Massachusetts)

[The following sections of the diary, beginning in August and ending September 1, 1843, are from the newly-discovered manuscript found in Walpole, New Hampshire, and never before published.]

and he brought his son James with him when Lizzy and I came home from our walk we played a little. After supper I played some again and then went to bed, having spent a very pleasant day.

Friday 4 [August]—After breakfast I washed the dishes and then had my lessons. Father and Mr. Ray and Mr. Lane went to the Shakers and did not return till evening.* After my lessons I sewed till dinner. When dinner was

---

* This visit was also noted in the Harvard Shaker Society Journal as follows: "August 1843 . . . Frid 4 Clear and pleasant. Finished mowing our grass this A.M. Get in the hay from the Haskel and White Meddows Two men by the names of Alcott & Lane (Transcendentalest) and a man from Philadelphia came here took dinner and stayed till towards night They seem to be inquiring into our principles . . . ."

over I had a bath, and then went to Mrs. Willards. When I came home I played till supper time, after which I read a little in Oliver Twist, and when I had thought a little I went to bed. I have spent quite a pleasant day.

Saturday 5—I rose early, and after breakfast I did the morning work; I had my lessons. I set the dinner table. After dinner, I had a bath and then went berrying, when I came home, I went to ride with Mother and Abba; when I returned I had my supper, and then went to bed.

Tuesday 8—After I had bathed and dressed, I came to breakfast. After breakfasting I washed the dishes and then went berrying with Anna and William we did not return untill dinner time. After dinner, I read and made clothes for my doll and had a bath. I sewed till 5 oclock, and went to walk. Lizzy and played out till supper was ready. After supper I washed the dishes, and went to bed.

Thursday 10—I rose early. After we had done breakfast I did my morning work. Father, Mother, Abba and Mr. Lane went to Leominster. I ironed a little and read till dinner was ready. After dinner I bathed. Lizzy William and I went blackberrying. Mother and Father came home in the evening. Though it was unpleasant without I was happy within.

*   *   *

hay and took care of Abba till supper after which I read a little and then went to bed.

Sunday 28—After breakfast I read till 9 Oclock and Father read a Parable called Nalhan and I like it very well he than asked us all what faults we wanted to get rid of I said Impatience and Mr. Lane selfwill. We had a dinner of bread and water after which I read thought and walked till supper.

Monday 29th—I rose at half past 4 and bathed and dressed had my singing lesson After breakfast I had my lessons after which I helped about dinner—in the afternoon I played and read.

Wednesday 30—After breakfast I washed

the dishes and then Mother Anna, Miss Robie and Harriet and myself went to Leominster to see a house which Father thinks of buying I liked it pretty well and I enjoyed my ride very much we did not return till evening.

Thursday 31—I had my lessons as usual and played till dinner after which I went to Mrs. Dudleys and did not return till supper time.

September 1843

Friday 1—I had my lessons as usual and Mr. Lane made a piece of poetry about Pestalossi I will put in

To Pestalozzi

On Pestalozzis sacred brow
The modest chesnut wreath
Green yesterday but fadeing now
And pasing as a breath.

Mother made up this piece—which I like very much

[The following entries, dated September through December 10, were copied and published by Mrs. Cheney. The originals have since been lost. The first entry date, September 1, may be an error of Mrs. Cheney's, since the Walpole manuscript shows a different entry for that date.]

September 1st—I rose at five and had my bath. I love cold water! Then we had our singing-lesson with Mr. Lane. After breakfast I washed dishes, and ran on the hill till nine and had some thoughts—it was so beautiful up there. Did my lessons—wrote and spelt and did sums; and Mr. Lane read a story, "The Judicious Father." How a rich girl told a poor girl not to look over the fence at the flowers, and was cross to her because she was unhappy. The Father heard her do it, and made the girls change clothes. The poor one was glad to do it, and he told her to keep them. But the rich one was very sad; for she had to wear the old ones a week, and after that she was good to shabby girls. I liked it very much, and I shall be kind to poor people.

Father asked us what was God's noblest work. Anna said *men*, but I said *babies*. Men are often bad; babies never are. We had a long talk, and I felt better after it, and *cleared up*.

We had bread and fruit for dinner. I read and walked and played till supper-time. We sung in the evening. As I went to bed the moon came up very brightly and looked at me. I felt sad because I have been cross to-day, and did not mind Mother. I cried, and then I felt better, and said that piece from Mrs. Sigourney, "I must not tease my mother." I get to sleep saying poetry—I know a great deal.

Thursday, 14th—Mr. Parker Pillsbury came, and we talked about the poor slaves. I had a music lesson with Miss P. I hate her, she is so fussy. I ran in the wind and played be a horse, and had a lovely time in the woods with Anna and Lizzie. We were fairies, and made gowns and paper wings. I "flied" the highest of all. In the evening they talked about travelling. I thought about Father going to England, and said this piece of poetry I found in Byron's poems:—

"When I left thy shores, O Naxos,
  Not a tear in sorrow fell;
Not a sigh or faltered accent
  Told my bosom's struggling swell."

It rained when I went to bed and made a pretty noise on the roof.

Sunday, 24th—Father and Mr. Lane have gone to N.H. to preach. It was very lovely . . . . Anna and I got supper. In the eve I read "Vicar of Wakefield." I was cross to-day, and I cried when I went to bed. I made good resolutions, and felt better in my heart. If I only *kept* all I make, I should be the best girl in the world. But I don't, and so am very bad.

(Poor little sinner! She says the same at fifty. —L.M.A.)

October 8th—When I woke up, the first thought I got was, "It's Mother's birthday: I must be very good." I ran and wished her a happy birthday, and gave her my kiss. After breakfast we gave her our presents. I had a moss cross and a piece of poetry for her.

We did not have any school, and played in

the woods and got red leaves. In the evening we danced and sung, and I read a story about "Contentment." I wish I was rich, I was good, and we were all a happy family this day.

We sang the following song:

Song of May

Hail, all hail, thou merry month of May,
We will hasten to the woods away
Among the flowers so sweet and gay,
Then away to hail the merry merry May—
    The merry merry May—
Then away to hail the merry merry month
    of May.

Hark, hark, hark, to hail the month of May,
How the songsters warble on the spray,
And we will be as blith as they,
Then away to hail the merry merry May—
Then away to hail the merry merry month
    of May.

I think this is a very pretty song and we sing it a good deal.

Thursday, 12th—After lessons I ironed. We all went to the barn and husked corn. It was good fun. We worked till eight o'clock and had lamps. Mr. Russell came. Mother and Lizzie are going to Boston. I shall be very lonely without dear little Betty, and no one will be as good to me as Mother. I read in Plutarch. I made a verse about sunset:—

"Softly doth the sun descend
    To his couch behind the hill,
Then, oh, then, I love to sit
    On mossy banks beside the rill."

Anna thought it was very fine; but I did n't like it very well.

Friday, Nov. 2nd—Anna and I did the work. In the evening Mr. Lane asked us, "What is man?" These were our answers: A human being; an animal with a mind; a creature; a body; a soul and a mind. After a long talk we went to bed very tired.

(No wonder, after doing the work and worrying their little wits with such lessons. —L.M.A.)

A sample of the vegetarian wafers used at Fruitlands:—

Vegetable diet
and sweet repose.
Animal food and
nightmare.

Pluck your body
from the orchard;
do not snatch it
from the shamble.

Without flesh diet
there could be no
blood-shedding war.

Apollo eats no
flesh and has no
beard; his voice is
melody itself.

Snuff is no less snuff
though accepted from
a gold box.

Tuesday, 20th—I rose at five, and after breakfast washed the dishes, and then helped mother work. Miss P. is gone, and Anna in Boston with Cousin Louisa. I took care of Abba (May) in the afternoon. In the evening I made some pretty things for my dolly. Father and Mr. L. had a talk, and father asked us if *we* saw any reason for us to separate. Mother wanted to, she is so tired. I like it, but not the school part or Mr. L.

Eleven years old. Thursday, 29th—It was Father's and my birthday. We had some nice presents. We played in the snow before school. Mother read "Rosamond" when we sewed. Father asked us in the eve what fault troubled us most. I said my bad temper.

I told mother I liked to have her write in my book. She said she would put in more and she wrote this to help me:—

"Dear Louey,—Your handwriting improves very fast. Take pains and do not be in a hurry. I like to have you make observations about our conversations and your own thoughts. It helps you to express them and to understand your little self. Remember, dear girl, that a diary should be an epitome of your life. May it be a record of pure thought and good actions, then you will indeed be the precious child of your loving mother."

—75—

December 10th—I did my lessons, and walked in the afternoon. Father read to us in dear "Pilgrim's Progress." Mr. L. was in Boston and we were glad. In the eve father and mother and Anna and I had a long talk. I was very unhappy, and we all cried. Anna and I cried in bed, and I prayed God to keep us all together.

[The following additional entries from the Walpole manuscript begin in December and continue to Christmas, 1843. The poems at the end are undated.]

spoken unkindly to the children and been disobedient to mother and father.

Saturday 23 [December]—In the morning mother went to the Village and I had my lessons and then helped Annie get dinner after which mother came home and Annie went on errand for mother to Mr. Lovejoye we stayed a little while to see their little baby boy I often wish I had a little brother but as I have not I shall try to be contented with what I have got, (for Mother often says, if we are not contented with what we have got it will be taken away from us) and I think it is very true. When we returned from Mr. Lovejoys, we played till supper time in the evening we played cards and when I went to bed I felt happy for I had been obedient and kind to Father and Mother and gentle to my sisters, I wish I could be gentle always.

Sunday 24th—After breakfast Father started for Boston, When he was gone I read and wrote till dinner after which I washed the dishes and then, I made some presents for Christmas in the evening I read and Mr. Palmer came and brought his son Thomas I did not go to bed till 10 oclock.

Christmas Day 1843

Monday 25—I rose early and sat some looking at the Bonbons in my stocking this is the piece of poetry which mother wrote for me.

CHRISTMASS RIMES

Christmass is here
  Louisa my dear
Then happy we'll be
  Gladsome and free
God with you abide
  With love for your guide
In time you'l go right
  With heart and with might.

This is a song which she sang soon after she began to travil to the Beatiful City.

1

Bless'd be the day that I began
  A Pilgrim for to be;
And blessed also be that man
  That there to moved me.
'Tis twice 'twas long ere I began
  To seek to live for ever;
But now I run fast as I can,
  'Tis better late than never.
Our tears to joy, our fears to faith,
  Are turned, as we see;
Thus our beginning (as one earth)
  Shows what our end will be.

1

What danger is the Pilgrim in,
    How many are his foes?
How many ways there are to sin,
    No living mortal knows.

2

Some in the ditch are spoiled; yea can
    Lie tumbling in the mire;
Some, though they shun the frying pan
    Do leap into the fire.

Here is an other

Behold ye how these crystal streams do glide
To comfort pilgrims, by the highway side,
The meadows green, besides their fragrant
                    smell
Yield dainties for them and he who can tell
What pleasant fruit, yea, leaves, these trees
                    do yield
Will soon sell all, that he may buy this field.

This is the sheepard boys song as he was
tending his fathers in the Vally of Humilition

1

He that is down needs fear no fall;
   He that low no pride;
He that is humble ever shall
   Have God to be his guide.

2

I am content with what I have.
   Little be it or much,
And Lord! contentment still I crave
   Because thou savest such.

Two Contemporary Letters

from Bronson Alcott and Charles Lane

A. Bronson Alcott
(Courtesy of the Fruitlands Museums, Harvard, Massachusetts)

WE HAVE MADE AN ARRANGEMENT WITH THE proprietor of an estate of about a hundred acres, which liberates this tract from human ownership. For picturesque beauty both in the near and the distant landscape, the spot has few rivals. A semi-circle of undulating hills stretches from south to west, among which the Wachusett and Monadnoc are conspicuous. The vale, through which flows a tributary to the Nashua, is esteemed for its fertility and ease of cultivation, is adorned with groves of nut-trees, maples, and pines, and watered by small streams. Distant not thirty miles from the metropolis of New England, this reserve lies in a serene and sequestered dell. No public thoroughfare invades it, but it is entered by a private road. The nearest hamlet is that of Stillriver, a field's walk of twenty minutes, and the village of Harvard is reached by circuitous and hilly roads of nearly three miles.

Here we prosecute our effort to initiate a Family in harmony with the primitive instincts in man. The present buildings being ill placed and unsightly as well as inconvenient, are to be temporarily used, until suitable and tasteful buildings in harmony with the natural scene can be completed. An excellent site offers itself on the skirts of the nearest wood, affording shade and shelter, and commanding a view of the lands of the estate, nearly all of which are capable of spade culture. It is intended to adorn the pastures with orchards, and to supersede ultimately the labor of the plough and cattle, by the spade and the pruning knife.

Our planting and other works, both without and within doors, are already in active progress. The present Family numbers ten individuals, five being children of the founders. Ordinary secular farming is not our object. Fruit, grain, pulse, garden plants and herbs, flax and other vegetable products for food, raiment, and domestic uses, receiving assiduous attention, afford at once ample manual occupation, and chaste supplies for the bodily needs. Consecrated to human freedom, the land awaits the sober culture of devout men.

Beginning with small pecuniary means, this enterprise must be rooted in a reliance on the succors of an ever bounteous Providence, whose vital affinities being secured by this union with uncorrupted fields and unworldly persons, the cares and injuries of a life of gain are avoided.

The inner nature of every member of the Family is at no time neglected. A constant leaning on the living spirit within the soul should consecrate every talent to holy uses, cherishing the widest charities. The choice Library (of which a partial catalogue was given in Dial No. XII.) is accessible to all who are desirous of perusing these records of piety and wisdom. Our plan contemplates all such disciplines, cultures, and habits, as evidently conduce to the purifying and edifying of the inmates. Pledged to the spirit alone, the founders can anticipate no hasty or numerous accession to their numbers. The kingdom of peace is entered only through the gates of self-denial and abandonment; and felicity is the test and the reward of obedience to the unswerving law of Love.

A. Bronson Alcott,
Charles Lane.

[from *The Dial*, July 1843]

OUR REMOVAL TO THIS ESTATE IN HUMBLE CON-
fidence has drawn to us several practical coad-
jutors, and opened many inquiries by letter for a
statement of our principles and modes of life. We
cannot perhaps turn our replies to better account
than to transcribe some portions of them for your
information, and, we trust, for your sincere satisfaction.

. . . We have not yet drawn out any preor-
dained plan of daily operations, as we are impressed
with the conviction that by a faithful reliance on
the spirit which actuates us, we are sure of attaining
to clear revelations of daily practical duties as they
are to be daily done by us. Where the Spirit of Love
and Wisdom abounds, literal forms are needless,
irksome or hinderative; where the Spirit is lacking,
no preconceived rules can compensate. . . .

Hence our perseverance in efforts to attain simplicity in diet, plain garments, pure bathing, unsul-
lied dwellings, open conduct, gentle behavior, kindly sympathies, serene minds. These, and the several
other particulars needful to the true end of man's
residence on earth, may be designated the Family
Life. . . .

Trade we hope entirely to avoid at an early
day. As a nursery for many evil propensities it is
almost universally felt to be a most undesirable

course. Such needful articles as we cannot yet raise by our own hand labor from the soil, thus redeemed from human ownership, we shall endeavor to obtain by friendly exchanges, and, as nearly as possible, without the intervention of money.

Of all the traffic in which civilized society is involved, that of human labor is perhaps the most detrimental. From the state of serfdom to the receipt of wages may be a step in human progress; but it is certainly full time for taking a new step out of the hiring system.

Our outward exertions are in the first instance directed to the soil, and as our ultimate aim is to furnish an instance of self-sustaining cultivation without the subjugation of either men or cattle, or the use of foul animal manures, we have at the outset to encounter struggles and oppositions somewhat formidable. Until the land is restored to its pristine fertility by the annual return of its own green crops, as sweet and animating manures, the human hand and simple implement cannot wholly supersede the employment of machinery and cattle. —So long as cattle are used in agriculture, it is very evident that man will remain a slave, whether he be proprietor or hireling. The driving of cattle beyond their natural and pleasurable exertion; the waiting upon them as cook and chambermaid three parts of the year; the excessive labor of mowing, curing, and whose filthy ordures are used under the erroneous supposition of restoring lost fertility; disease is thus infused into the human body; stimulants and medicines are resorted to for relief, which end in a precipitation of the original evil to a more disastrous depth. These misfortunes which affect not only the body, but by reaction rise to the sphere of the soul, would be avoided, at least in part, by the disuse of animal food. Our diet is therefore strictly of the pure and bloodless kind. No animal substances, neither flesh, butter, cheese, eggs nor milk, pollute our tables or corrupt our bodies, neither tea, coffee, molasses, nor rice, tempts us beyond the bounds of indigenous productions. Our sole beverage is pure fountain water. The native grains, fruits, herbs and roots, dressed with the utmost cleanliness, and regard to their purpose of edifying a healthful body, furnish the pleasantest refections and in the greatest variety requisite to the supply of the various organs. The field, the orchard, the garden, in their bounteous products of wheat, rye, barley, maize, oats, buckwheat; apples, pears, peaches, plums, cherries, currants, berries; potatoes, peas, beans, beets, carrots, melons, and other vines, yield an ample store for human nutrition, without dependence on foreign climes, or the degradations of shipping and trade. The almost inexhaustible variety which the several stages and sorts of vegetable growth, and the several modes of preparation afford, are a full answer to the question which is often put by those who have never ventured into the region of a pure and chaste diet: "If you give up flesh meat, upon what then can you live?"

Our other domestic habits are in harmony with those of diet. We rise with early dawn, begin the day with cold bathing, succeeded by a music lesson, and then a chaste repast. Each one finds occupation until the meridian meal, when usually some interesting and deep-searching conversation gives rest to the body and development to the mind. Occupation, according to the season and the weather, engages us out of doors or within, until the evening meal,—when we again assemble in social communion, prolonged generally until sunset, when we resort to sweet repose for the next day's activity.

In these steps of reform we do not rely as much on scientific reasoning or physiological skill, as on the Spirit's dictates. The pure soul, by the law in its own nature, adopts a pure diet and cleanly customs; nor needs detailed instruction for daily conduct. On a revision of our proceedings it would seem, that if we were in the right course in our particular instance, the greater part of man's duty consists in leaving alone much that he is in the habit of doing. It is a fasting from the present activity, rather

than an increased indulgence in it, which, with patient watchfulness, tends to newness of life. Shall I
sip tea or coffee? the inquiry may be. No. Abstain
from *all* ardent, as from alcoholic drinks. Shall I
consume pork, beef, or mutton? Not if you value
health or life. Shall I stimulate with milk? No. Shall
I warm my bathing water? Not if cheerfulness is
valuable. Shall I clothe in many garments? Not if
purity is aimed at. Shall I prolong my dark hours,
consuming animal oil and losing bright daylight in
the morning? Not if a clear mind is an object. Shall
I teach my children the dogmas inflicted on myself,
under the pretense that I am transmitting truth?
Nay, if you love them intrude not these between
them and the Spirit of all Truth. Shall I subjugate
cattle? Shall I trade? Shall I claim property in any
created thing? Shall I interest myself in politics? To
how many of these questions, could we ask them
deeply enough, could they be heard as having relation to our eternal welfare, would the response be
"Abstain"? Be not so active to do, as sincere to *be*.
Being in preference to doing, is the great aim, and
this comes to us rather by a resigned willingness
than a wilful activity; which is indeed a check to all
divine growth. Outward abstinence is a sign of inward fulness; and the only source of true progress is
inward. We may occupy ourselves actively in
human improvements;—but these unless inwardly

well-impelled, never attain to, but rather hinder, divine progress in man. During the utterance of this narrative it has undergone some change in its personal expression which might offend the hypercritical; but we feel assured that you will kindly accept it as the unartful offering of both your friends in ceaseless aspiration.

CHARLES LANE,
A. BRONSON ALCOTT.

[from a letter published in the *Herald of Freedom*, September 8, 1843] housing hay, and of collecting other fodder, and the large extra quantity of land needful to keep up this system, forms a combination of unfavorable circumstances which must depress the humane affections, so long as it continues, and overlay them by the injurious and extravagant development of the animal and bestial natures in man. It is calculated that if no animal food were consumed, one-fourth of the land now used would suffice for human sustenance. And the extensive tracts of country now appropriated to grazing, mowing, and other modes of animal provision, could be cultivated by and for intelligent and affectionate human neighbors. The sty and the stable too often secure more of the farmer's regard than he bestows on the garden and the children. No hope is there for humanity while woman is withdrawn from the tender assiduities which adorn her and her household, to the servitudes of the dairy and the flesh pots. If the beasts were wholly absent from man's neighborhood, the human population might be at least four times as dense as it now is without raising the price of land. This would give to the country all the advantages of concentration without the vices which always spring up in the dense city.

Debauchery of both the earthly soil and the human body is the result of this cattle keeping. The land is scourged for crops to feed the animals,